FEAR

Fear:
The Silent Killer of Church Growth!

by

Calvin C. Barlow Jr.

905 South Douglas Avenue • Nashville, Tennessee 37204
Phone: 615-972-2842
E-mail: Lowbarpublishingcompany@gmail.com
Web site: www.Lowbarbookstore.com

Copyright © 2016 Calvin C. Barlow Jr.

No part of this book may be reproduced or transmitted in any form or by any means—graphic, electronic, or mechanical, including photocopying, recording, taping, or by any information storage retrieval system—without the permission, in writing, of the publisher or author.

Lowbar Publishing Company
905 S. Douglas Ave.
Nashville, Tennessee 37204
615-972-2842
Lowbarpublishingcompany@gmail.com
www.Lowbarbookstore.com

Editor: Honey B. Higgins
Graphic and Cover Design Artist: Norah S. Branch

Unless otherwise noted, Scripture references in this book are taken from the King James Version of the Holy Bible.

Those marked NKJV are taken from the New King James Version®. Copyright © 1982 by Thomas Nelson. Used by permission. All rights reserved.

Printed in the United States of America.

ISBN: 978-0-9969432-1-5

For additional information or to contact the author for workshops or seminars, please use the phone number listed above.

Table of Contents

Foreword..vii

Introduction...viii

Chapter 1   Exposing the Fear of Leadership 1

Chapter 2   Church Killers.. 11

Chapter 3   Overcoming the Fear of Leadership 22

Chapter 4   Turning Church Killers into Life Givers........................... 26

Chapter 5   Building the Team 33

Chapter 6   A Paradigm for Church Growth.. 41

Chapter 7   When Fear Stagnates Church Growth.............................. 56

Appendices 61

    A. Glossary of Terminology

    B. Twelve Things that Hinder Church Growth

    C. A Church Demographic Survey

    D. Church Myths that Hinder Church Growth

    E. Five Principles of the Great Commission

    F. A Personal Observation of Church Trends

    G. Other Church Growth Resources

    H. Other Books by the Author

Foreword

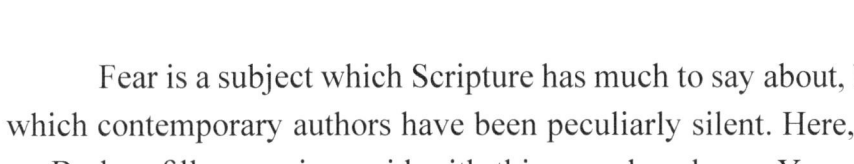

Fear is a subject which Scripture has much to say about, but on which contemporary authors have been peculiarly silent. Here, Bishop Barlow fills a gaping void with this superb volume. You will be challenged and encouraged as you read. If there is a spark of spiritual desire in your soul, this book will surely kindle it into a blazing passion to deal with your fear.

Cordell E. Simpson I, Pastor

Eighth Street Missionary Baptist Church

Introduction

Not every church will be a mega- or giga-church, but every church should consist of a growing congregation. A *mega-church* is defined as a congregation that has one thousand or more members. A *giga-church* is defined as a congregation that has ten thousand or more members. The term "giga-church" is said to have been coined by Bill Easum. Around 2007, according to some church statisticians, approximately thirty-six churches within the United States had at least ten thousand people in weekly worship. However, the average membership size for a Christian congregation, in America, is approximately 180 members. Yet, at least one half of all churches in America have seventy-five or less members.

There is new data defining mega- and giga-churches based upon their weekly worship attendance. Accordingly, a *mega-church* is defined as a congregation that has at least two thousand or more weekly worshippers in attendance. A giga-church has at least ten thousand or more weekly worshippers in attendance. Unfortunately, too many congregations are having little or no growth. The question has to be asked, "What is the cause for this obvious growth stagnation?"

- Is it because people are moving their membership to mega-churches?
- Is it because there aren't any more people that need to be saved?
- Is it because there aren't any more unchurched people?

An unchurched person falls into two categories. Some people are considered unchurched because they have not accepted Jesus Christ as their personal Savior. Some people are considered to be unchurched because they are not faithfully attending a specific congregation for worship and spiritual growth. In other words, they are saved but wandering as lost sheep. Unchurched people are like those persons over whom Jesus prophesied. He saw them as sheep without a shepherd (Mark 6:34). Yet! the question is, "Why don't some congregations grow numerically?" Even though there are reports of cannibalization among mega- and giga-churches, the question remains. There are those who declare that the fasting-growing churches are those that have a membership in excess of five thousand members. On the other hand, there are indicators that people, in this century, are disconnecting and refusing to connect with churches, especially traditional congregations. Thus, the church finds itself in some ways dealing with the opportunities of the ancient church. Yet, many smaller congregations fail to take advantage of a world that is searching for purity of faith.

Acts 2:41 states that in one day, about three thousand people were added to the church. The second chapter of the book of Acts concludes by stating that people were added to the church as the Lord saw the need. Perhaps some congregations do not grow because its leaders believe that God has preordained which congregation shall grow and which congregation shall not grow. Often when things do not live up to our expectations, we find a word to shield us from personal failure. The fact is this: we are to win souls for Christ. Christ does not place a quota on the quantity of souls to be won. He tells us to win souls. The writer Matthew closed his gospel with Christ's appeal for us to *go*. We are to win souls. Yes, some congregations may win more than others. However, every congregation ought to be winning some souls.

The Bible states, "The harvest is plentiful but the laborers are few" (see Matthew 9:37). This implies that the amount of labor put forth determines the yield of the harvest.

Some people make the argument that many congregations do not grow because they are stuck in the past and that is the reason why they do not grow. Yet! methodology and doctrine are not the same. There are congregations whose doctrine is conservative but that have more members than smaller congregations with what is called the liberty doctrine. Too many small congregations believe that changing their name or changing their doctrine will cause more people to join their congregation. In many instances, these congregations lose their identity and never achieve a sufficient increase in membership. This is called the fishing-hole syndrome. The *fishing-hole syndrome* is based upon the act of a non-fisherman moving from his or her fishing spot to the spot where other fishermen are catching fish—believing that the changing of location will produce caught fish. Therefore, some small congregations believe that if they just do what the mega-congregations are doing that they will acquire more members. The non-fishermen never take into consideration that true fishermen take the time to learn about water depth, strike zones, weights, types of baits for types of fish, and the other things that make one a fisherman. Non-fishermen believe that all one needs to do is to cast the line into the water to catch fish. Thus, many small congregations believe that all you need to do is just open the church doors on Sundays and Wednesday nights and people will come.

Some congregations are not growing because the membership believes that it is the best means of maintaining their purity. Usually, these congregations have a belief that everybody is corrupt except them. The Bible reads, "All have sinned, and come short of the glory of God" (Romans 3:24). First John 1:8 reads, "If we say that we have no sin, we deceive ourselves, and the truth is not in us." This implies that sin is a constant in people waiting for the opportunity to perform. When a congregation becomes an exclusive club for some people, it is not maintaining purity but operating in fear.

There are many reasons for church growth problems. However, one of the fundamental causes is fear. Fear suffocates church growth. The Bible warns us about the spirit of fear and even informs us about its author. The spirit of fear is not of God but it is the tool of the devil. In order for a congregation to be a growing congregation, it must deal with fear. Fear comes in all sizes and shapes. In other words, fear knows how to disguise itself. Fear knows how to dress up and speak with sophisticated words. Fear knows how to veil itself with worldly honors. Fear knows God's Word but refuses to submit to the principles of God's Word.

A congregation's buying the latest evangelism manual will not grow it if that congregation does not deal with its fear challenges. In order for methodology to work effectively, two things are required: conviction and the willingness to face the unknown. In other words, if a congregation is not convinced that evangelism grows a congregation, then their buying evangelism manuals will not change the outcome. And on the same hand, if a congregation does not have the willingness to deal with the unknown, it will retreat from the manual's proven theories. I am amazed at the number of evangelism classes taught in church associations, Christian education congresses, and local congregations. Yet, for the most part, less than 20 percent of church growth (in America) is the outgrowth of biblical evangelism. The twenty-first-century church growth model seems to be motivated by "status seekers, cannibalization, and a club mentality." For instance, there are persons who move their membership to a certain congregation because it adds perceived status to their identity. On the other hand, according to data, there are congregations that create methodologies and programs for the sole purpose of consuming other congregations' membership. Finally, there are those persons who love to be in the crowd. Crowd seekers have a club mentality.

Christians are called to be truth proclaimers. Yet, in many instances, we prevent the Holy Spirit from doing His job. One of the job descriptions of the Holy Spirit is "Persuader in Chief." In other words, it is the job of the Holy Spirit to convict people of the truth.

> "But now I go away to Him who sent Me, and none of you asks Me, 'Where are You going?' But because I have said these things to you, sorrow has filled your heart. Nevertheless I tell you the truth. It is to your advantage that I go away; for if I do not go away, the Helper will not come to you; but if I depart, I will send Him to you. And when He has come, He will convict the world of sin, and of righteousness, and of judgment: of sin, because they do not believe in Me; of righteousness, because I go to My Father and you see Me no more; of judgment, because the ruler of this world is judged." (John 16:5-11, NKJV)

However, if we (Christians) fail to proclaim truth, the Holy Spirit cannot convict people of the truth. Yet, many times we fail to speak truth because of fear. Sometimes, we hold the truth rather than sharing the truth out of the fear of negative repercussions. In moments like these, we find comfort in saying, "It's in God's hands." Sometimes, we attempt to place in God's hands that which He has placed in our hands for action. This is the excuse that the man with one talent made: "Lord, because of who you are, I decided to hide the money you gave me rather than to trust the marketplace" (see

Matthew 25:14-30)—rather than saying, "Lord, I need help with my fear." The man committed an act, out of fear, as though he was doing God a favor. Fear leads one to lie to self as well as to God.

The premise of this work is to identify fear as one of the root causes that prevents a congregation from growing. Whereas this work does not claim fear to be the only thing that prevents congregational growth, it is one of the leading reasons. Taking ownership of fear is not easy. A person whose bookkeeping skills are limited to a paper ledger system will not say, "The reason I don't want a computerized bookkeeping system is because of the fear of losing my job." Fear leads us to justify logistical lies.

Fear robs the present of its prophetic past while closing the door to its futuristic purpose. Fear is a train wreck in action. One's taking ownership of his or her fear is the beginning of growth. A baby does not learn how to walk until he or she takes ownership of the fear of falling.

In this work, we will look behind some forbidden doors because sometimes fear lingers in places that we deem to be off-limits. However, if a congregation is to be a growing congregation then no position within the congregation can be off-limits. Fear has no respect of positions. Elijah seemed to have had no fear in fighting Baal's prophets but ran from Jezebel. In other words, sometimes leadership can stand against many and flee from few.

The facts are these: everyone in a position of leadership within a congregation and its members is vulnerable to fear. Fear is one of the main reasons for church division. Fear is a polarizer that knocks at the doors of kings, pastors, deacons, and members with the same vengeance. Failure to acknowledge fear is to allow its presence into sacred places.

In this work, we will seek to expose fear in every cavity. As we expose fear's grip, we will provide tools for overcoming fear. It is not the purpose of this work to surrender to fear but, rather, to defeat it, and manage its presence in everyday living. Congregations cannot grow effectively until they deal with the challenges of fear. Christians are overcomers. All things are possible with and through God. The ultimate goal of this work is to see every congregation that is established by Christ achieving its divine purpose.

Reflective and Critical Thinking

Discussion Questions:

- ❖ How do we get church members to buy into the validity of evangelism?

- ❖ What challenges do congregations face in relation to evangelism?

- ❖ Are congregations using outdated methods as it relates to twenty-first-century evangelistic needs?

- ❖ Do our leadership teams understand the role of the Holy Spirit as it relates to evangelism success?

- ❖ Do our leadership teams understand the difference between the "pitch person" and "the closer" as it relates to evangelism?

Chapter 1

Exposing the Fear of Leadership

The Pastor

When an airplane crashes or disappears, the first persons to be investigated are usually the pilot and co-pilot. They are the people in authority. Likewise when a church is not growing, the pastor must submit to a process of self-investigation. Just as the cockpit is to be kept safe at all times from unqualified and unauthorized persons, so is the pulpit's authority. While congregations' by-laws may vary, there are several factors that are biblical when it comes to the authority of the pulpit:

- ➢ Who preaches;
- ➢ Doctrinal teachings; and
- ➢ The worship moment.

The pastor needs to make sure that the pulpit's authority has not been compromised by fear.

Some pastors believe that their position protects them from fear. This is wishful thinking and it undermines the pastor's authority in every arena of leadership.

> *A young pastor is called to pastor a historic church. His predecessor died after being with the congregation for forty-four years. Within one month, the former pastor's wife moves her membership. And within six months, the young pastor changes the church's external fellowships and its internal polity. He does this upon the premise that he is the pastor and the congregation is to follow him and not what they did under the previous pastor.*

Pastors have the authority to lead congregations. Yet, sometimes leadership is cloaked in fear. Some pastors are always fighting the ghost of the last pastor and sometimes give life to undeserved skeletons. When fear disguises itself as leadership, it is known as the "Jeroboam syndrome." Jeroboam's decision to build a place of worship in Samaria had nothing to do with the people's safety and the travel distance to Jerusalem. He feared that if they continued to go to Jerusalem to worship then he would lose their loyalty. When change is used to disconnect people from their pasts, this decision need not to have been made as a result of fear. Leadership needs to be free of fear because sometimes a disconnection is needed in order to go forth.

Fear can lead leaders down a path of being too cautious.

> *A senior pastor has a feeding program. The program was the vision of the pastor, and two culinary persons of the church volunteer to be the cooks. Later the*

pastor sees the need to expand the ministry, but the cooks disagree with the pastor's vision to expand the ministry. After some time, the pastor replaces the cooks with new cooks. The previous cooks become irate and wreak havoc in other areas of the church life that have nothing to do with the feeding ministry. Members of the church make known to the pastor the problems being created by the disgruntled cooks. However, the pastor believes that he needs to move slowly with corrective actions. After all, the cooks are financial supporters of the church and have family members and friends within the congregation. Therefore, the pastor justified his handling of the situation by saying, "Church members are like tree roots. You don't know how they are entangled."

It is wise to be cautious, but being too cautious is an excuse to do nothing. Fear knows that if we do nothing when doing something is required, then our doing nothing will stagnate growth. Being too cautious is like planting a seed and not watering it because of the fear of overwatering it. Many congregations have had good planting seasons but are not growing because leadership is too cautious to adequately water what has been planted.

Sometimes fear portrays itself as being humble and meek. Christ was humble and meek, but He was not passive. When humility and meekness produce passive leadership, it is leadership without authority. Authoritarian leadership gives the leader the right to act.

A pastor is called to his first church and the church's clerk is the record keeper of the financial records of the church. Each Sunday, the church's clerk records the

> *funds of the church but refuses to share the information with the pastor. The pastor believes that he needs this information to make recommendations for the funding of church ministries. He is often told by the church's clerk that the church cannot fund his recommendations of some ministries due to the lack of funds. Because this is the church history of handling its financial affairs, the pastor does not say anything.*

When leadership goes along just to get along, it is being guided by fear. When fear produces a humble and meek spirit, it is called *passivity*. Passivity is fear disguised with a smile. A passive leadership style is known as being one to not "rock the boat." This type of leadership robs leaders of their rightful authority and the congregation suffers.

Some leaders are led to believe that some fights do not need to be fought. This type of thinking fails to realize the purpose of leadership. Leaders are not called to fight; leaders are called to protect, provide for, and motivate a designated group of people. Fear understands psychology.

> *A church school teacher uses a classroom to attack a deacon's leadership. Sunday after Sunday, the teacher finds ways to attack the deacon. The pastor is made known of the inappropriate use of classroom time. The pastor believes that the distraction is personal and, therefore, refuses to speak to the teacher. When asked why he has not spoken to the teacher, he says, "Some things God has to take care of."*

Sometimes fear causes leaders to hide their authority as though God has not equipped their authority with power. God does not give authority to leaders to be hidden; He gives authority to leaders to act. Leaders are not called to hide but to stand.

Fear is like carbon monoxide: sometimes it has you in its death grip before it is detected.

> *A pastor—for whatever reason—has a problem with holding certain persons of the ministerial staff accountable. For some unknown reason and justifiable notion, it is his belief that persons respond better when they are not pressed to be accountable. Without being aware of the implication of the decision, fear has the pastor practicing partially among the membership.*

It might be that the pastor does not want to hurt the feelings of persons. It might be that the pastor feels that these persons do not have the capacity to grow in ministry. Yet the pastor, from time to time, allows these persons to perform ministerial duties. However, the pastor has no problem with stating that the choir member who misses rehearsal cannot sing in the choir. The pastor's decision to hold some leaders accountable and to allow other leaders to do as they wish leaves the church's members in a conundrum. Partiality is fear cloaked in fondness and tempered with bias.

There are pastors who make the statement, "Those people don't want to move." Sometimes fear shows up as a comforter for what appears to be a hopeless situation.

> *A pastor is called to a historical rural church. The church has had multiple pastors in its lengthy history. In its heyday, fifty years ago, its seventy-five-member seating capacity was filled each Sunday. It was the place where teachers and landowners came to pray, fellowship, and*

play. It had the best baseball team. Its members prepared the best fellowship dinners. Children crafted the art of public speaking while standing nervously before their peers. The remnant of this once-great church loves to brag about their prolific past while closing their eyes to an empty present. The membership has gotten older, with a few middle-aged members who work each day. Their children have gone to colleges to find distance jobs and in the hopes of finding love and marriage. Grandchildren only visit during holidays and summer breaks. A once-robust ministry has been reduced to Sunday morning worship and summertime Bible study, sprinkled with a "whenever" Sunday school. The new pastor goes to church each Sunday but he goes with the thought, "Those people don't want to move."

Fear is a prophesier of failure. Fear is a first cousin to "doom'sday philosophers." Fear knows that one of the best ways to defeat kingdom building is to create a spirit of defeat. A spirit of defeat produces a "don't care" attitude. People give in and give out easier when they have no commitment to the task at hand. It is unfortunate that some pastors prophesy their failure before they attempt to succeed. A noncommittal attitude allows a congregation to rest on the laurels of yesterday's efforts. Fear knows how to comfort frustration—it is called *detachment*. And where there is detachment, there is a lack of interest. A lack of interest produces non-committal leadership. Just because the congregation does not care does not justify the leadership to go AWOL.

Fear has its ways of diminishing leadership. Fear is the opposite of courage. Therefore, to be brave is to face your fear. You cannot overcome fear until you acknowledge its presence. Fear does not behave the same way under every condition. Sometimes fear will cause a person to smile, and sometimes it will cause a person to be talkative. Fear negotiates decisions: *Should I or shouldn't I?* Fear is a norm but it is destructive if not acknowledged and controlled. Therefore, when a congregation is not growing, the pastor needs to conduct a self-evaluation. Once the pastor has acknowledged personal fear and taken proactive means to control its effects, the pastor is free to bring forth methods of moving the church into a growth mode.

Every church is to be a growing congregation. If a congregation has twenty-five members, and it adds five members within a year, it would have increased its membership by 20 percent. Every church should be actively winning souls for the kingdom of God.

> *Fishermen will tell you that not every species of fish is attracted to the same bait. Therefore, not every potential soul for the kingdom is attracted to a mega- or giga-congregation.*

We are called to be fishers of men. We are not called to admire others at the expense of neglecting the opportunity to be kingdom builders.

The pastor has a grave responsibility. The author of the spirit of fear is cognitive of the pastor's task. Fear seeks to be disruptive in every arena that deals with pastoral authority. Fear knows that if the pastor is entangled in personal fear, then pulpit authority is compromised. When pulpit authority is compromised, church killers are free to wreak havoc among the congregation. Therefore, it is imperative that the pastor acknowledge personal fear and subdue it with the help of the Holy Spirit. God does not leave His leaders helpless against the venom of the enemy. The pastor has to stay suited at all times for warfare. The enemy does not take a time-out or vacation.

Other Leaders

The pastor is not the only leader in the congregation. The devil is aware that there are other leaders in the congregation. Some are named to appointed positions, and others are not. Thus, fear can be used as a divisive force to stagnate church growth among these subordinated leaders. Fear is the common denominator that stagnates church growth regardless of the leader's position.

If pastors can be likened to pilots of an airplane, then the other positions of leadership within the congregation can be likened to stewards of an airplane. The stewardess or steward is to minister to the passengers. They are to take care of the passengers' incidental needs. They are to make sure that a passenger does not become a threat to others or to the safety of the airplane. Likewise, subordinated leaders within the congregation are to minister to the membership's needs. Deacons and trustees are to minister to the needs of the membership. Ushers, directors, and greeters are to minister to the needs of the membership. Unfortunately, fear causes some persons in these subordinated leadership positions to abandon their purpose. When purpose is abandoned, it causes stress in other areas of the church's life. When the congregation has to deal with unanticipated stress, it loses focus of its divine purpose—which is to win souls for the kingdom of God.

The devil uses pride and other tactics to destroy the team concepts among church leaders.

> *A pastor is given a vision to build a new sanctuary, and the congregation votes to accept the vision of the pastor. For whatever reason, there are other subordinated leaders who cannot accept the sentiments of the people. Fear gives them a litany of things that is wrong with the vision. The subordinated leaders derail the building*

program. The church members are polarized and church growth ceases.

Fear is an equal-opportunity employer. Every leader in the congregation must face personal fear. When personal fear is left unchecked, it causes one to make unhealthy decisions.

The church's subordinated leaders are appointed to facilitate congregational growth. The church clerk's and the Minister of Music's job descriptions within the church may not include evangelism responsibilities, but they are to perform their duties in a manner that facilitates congregational growth. The chairperson of the deacon's ministry may not be a member of the evangelistic team, but the chairperson of deacons is to perform the duties of the deacon ministry in ways that facilitate congregational growth. Every church leader needs to ask himself, "How do I perform my assignment in a manner that promotes congregational growth?" Each church leader has to overcome fear in order to prevent growth stagnation and hindrances. Unfortunately, many subordinated leaders, and especially of smaller congregations, never discover their divine purpose. When church leaders are unaware of their divine purpose, they become disablers rather than enablers. While they may be ushering, they are ushers of reduction and not production. They may be choir members singing uplifting songs, but their actions are uplifting chaos and confusion. They may be trustees who maintain the church's facilities, yet sustain hell raising within the congregation. Fear is a divider. If left unchecked, fear will rearrange goals and objectives. Fear is a destabilizer. Fear is not a friend of righteousness. Fear is one of the devil's tools to prevent the growth of God's earthly kingdom, which is the church.

Reflective and Critical Thinking

Discussion Questions:

❖ Does our congregation have a tool that allows leadership the opportunity to evaluate itself?

❖ Do our leaders have written job descriptions?

❖ Does the congregation have short-term and long-term goals?

❖ Are auxiliary leaders encouraged to support the church's agenda?

❖ What does our congregation do to boost morale?

Chapter 2

Church Killers

Church killers are intentional or unintentional actions of persons that wreak havoc in the church. In some instances, the action is caused by a lack of wisdom. The action can be caused by a person or methodology. Whereas fear is not obvious and is often unseen, a church killer's tactics are blatant and noisy. The tactics are used by persons to demonstrate their influence over the membership. In some instances, the tactics are vindictive. Sometimes methodology wreaks havoc within the congregation. This is the truth of the Doctrine of Inclusivity. However, church killers' tactics have the same effect as fear—they both stagnate church growth. Many church killers operate under the notion that they are doing God a favor.

The Doctrine of Inclusivity

The Doctrine of Inclusivity is a method that seeks to include everybody in participation of something within a defined group of persons. When used in the church without wisdom, this doctrine can do more harm than good.

Sometimes, new members who are untrained and unfamiliar with congregational ethos are placed among the shark-minded people too quickly. In every congregation there are persons who live to annoy leaders. At other times, persons who have antiauthoritarian sentiments are placed in leadership positions.

It is most pastors' desire to have persons within the congregation participating in some type of ministry. However, placing untrained persons, agenda seekers, and new members in positions of leadership, just to be inclusive, can create shockwaves of unnecessary conflict within a congregation.

> *A pastor has twelve ministers on staff. In trying to include all of the ministers in the ministry of the congregation, he places one of the ministers as a teacher of a Young Adult class. The young minister is a very meek person, a tither, and he is very supportive of the pastor. However, his teaching skills are so notorious that some of the students stop coming to class. Once a growing class that was being used as a vehicle for church evangelism, it has now become the butt of the church's jokes.*

Just as placing untrained persons in a position for the sake of inclusion is not wise, so it is with placing people in positions of leadership who do not have the right attitude.

> *A pastor feels sorry for a person who possesses managerial skills but has notorious people skills—so he places that person in a directorial position. The pastor wants to include the person in ministry. The person*

> *immediately uses the position as a means to compete with other persons within the congregation. The person even becomes combative with the pastor about the vision and direction of the assigned ministry. Instead of championing the assigned ministry, the director seeks to kill the influence and function of the ministry.*

Many congregations and especially smaller congregations are not growing due to the mishandling of inclusivity. Even though the act of inclusivity is not intended to kill church growth, sometimes it does. Every person deserves the opportunity to participate in ministry. The question is, "When and where?" When inclusivity is used inappropriately, it becomes a church killer.

Servant leaders must ask the question, "Do we learn by practicing on people, or do we learn by preparing ourselves to practice on people?" Some small churches are producing a culture of growth stagnation by using new members, agenda seekers, and untrained, unteachable, and unprepared persons in its leadership positions.

Unhealthy Sentiments

Unhealthy sentiments are church killers. Unhealthy sentiments are strong feelings that hold a congregation to its past at the price of being unproductive.

> *A congregation built a facility ahead of its time. It was the icon of the community. However, over the last seventy-five years the community has changed. The membership has dwindled and the remaining members refuse to relocate or evangelize its new neighbors.*

When a sentiment of yesterday's memories prevents one from acknowledging a present reality, it is a church killer. When congregations find more pleasure in gathering over fellowship dinners than creating growth ministries, it is evidence of a congregation being tied to its past glory and not its current reality.

Many smaller churches and especially rural churches are not growing because there is a noisy and blatant group of people always attempting to shackle its members to the past. When unhealthy and unproductive sentiments prevail, a spirit of doom and hopelessness is created. When a congregation functions within the sphere of doom and hopelessness, church growth is stagnated.

Sometimes the sentiment is not tied to a location or building but is tied to an ideology or methodology. When sentiments are tied to ideology or methodology, they are called *traditions*. There is a difference between Bible doctrine, denominational dogma, and traditions. *Traditions*, within a congregation, are things that members believe or do which cannot be undergirded by a holistic interpretation of Scripture. The wearing of white gloves when servicing communion is a tradition. Walking or sitting when taking the communion is a tradition. Even standing when reading the Scripture is also a tradition. There are many traditions practiced among Christians. When ideology and methodology hinder a congregation from being relevant, they are church killers. Some small churches fail to grow because the membership spends more time debating traditions than studying and applying God's Word to their lives.

The Controller Syndrome

The *controller syndrome* is a dictatorial managerial style employed by a person to limit the input and assessment of a specified task by other persons within a defined group of people. The controller syndrome is a church killer. It robs members of the congregation of their spiritual gift potentiality. A church functions best when it uses the spiritual gifts of all of its members. However, in certain instances, there are persons who see their gift as the exclusive gift of a defined group of people. Controllers have a "takeover and go-it-alone" spirit. They are very opinionated and demanding, and sometimes use ultimatums to achieve their purpose. When a congregation is denied collective input, due to a controller's spirit agenda, church growth is stagnated.

> *A church is planning to have a fellowship dinner. The church has a member who is one of the best cooks in the city. The cook agrees to be responsible for the menu and preparation of the food. The person who is responsible for the décor and traffic flow suggested that the food be served in a location whereas to minimize congestion. The cook is an outstanding cook but has no work experience in event management. However, the cook feels that his influence is being threatened and refuses to prepare the food if the location is not changed. The event planner resigns her position due to the threats of the cook. Therefore, the congregation was denied the gifts of the event planner.*

The controller syndrome not only denies congregations of the possible spiritual gifts of the membership, but it stagnates church growth. People who desire to serve in ministry will not stay in congregations where certain members are allowed to control the assigned ministry without reasonable input from others.

The Resistance Syndrome

The *resistance syndrome* is a push-back tactic. The resistance syndrome is used by persons to keep leadership in line. The tactic is typically used against the pastor by subordinated leaders or disgruntled members. When used by subordinated leaders, it serves to cause unrest and confusion within the congregation in order to stop certain initiatives. Sometimes it is used to show that the pastor's effectiveness in the pastoral position is subjected to a lesser position. When used by disgruntled members, it is a vindictive means of getting back at leadership for a perceived wrong. Sometimes church members feel that they have been denied or looked over. When church members feel that they have been denied or looked over, they seize moments to get back at leadership. Often people find it difficult to communicate their perception of an offense and use resistance and complaints as means to massage their wounded feelings.

On the other hand, many subordinated leaders use resistance as a means to keep leaders off-guard. The tactic is usually a noisy and combative one. This tactic is a church killer. People do not want to be members of congregations where open hostility is the norm.

The Small-vision Syndrome

The *small-vision syndrome* is when people always see themselves as grasshoppers. These people always magnify the problems more than the promises of God. They have a fixation on problems but never have viable solutions for the problems that they claim are an obstacle for success. They are always telling people what cannot be done while claiming that they serve a God who can do all things. The small-vision person has a faith problem. These people always seek to hold the congregation back while robbing it of its possibilities due to their fear of the unknown. Because these people think small, they can never see a future of greatness. These people cannot multitask. They have a "tunnel vision" mentality. They are people who do not have a real relationship with a God of faith. They talk about faith but never exercise faith. The Word of God says that faith without works is dead (see James 2:20). Thus, these people are guilty of James's diagnosis—their faith has no works. These small-minded people have no trusting faith. When faith cannot produce works, it is ineffective faith. It is like having medicine to heal but not having the belief to take it.

> *A pastor has a plan to pay off a mortgage over the span of ten years. The pastor provides the church with a reasonable and achievable plan to accomplish the task. Yet, for some reason, certain persons refuse to apply faith and persuade others that it cannot be done.*

The small-vision syndrome is a church killer because it robs a congregation of its accessibility to God's power, which is through faith. When a congregation becomes comfortable with doing nothing, progressive members usually seek other places of worship.

The Undermining Syndrome

The *Undermining Syndrome* is a tactic used to produce failure. Of all of the church-killer tactics, this is the most dangerous and destructive in a congregation. This tactic is from the pits of hell. It is anti-leadership and seeks to disrupt the cohesiveness of the congregation. It is used by disgruntled and disfranchised members of the congregation. It is most effective when used by subordinate leaders of the congregation.

Unfortunately, in many congregations, people use failure to enhance their status within a membership. These people comprise the "I told you so" crowd. These people fight to keep the status quo for their own operational advantages. The tactic is dangerous because it uses darkness from the pits of hell to persuade members of a congregation to fight and undermine the pastoral leadership. The following is a list of tactics used in the undermining syndrome:

- Skelton's excavation
- Family's unity
- Financial manipulation
- Favoritism
- Exposure of ungodly habits

The Seed-eater Syndrome

Within the *Seed-eater Syndrome* is the seed eater—a person who seeks to consume all of the harvest's seeds rather than planting a seed for a greater harvest. This person is like the person who killed the goose that laid the golden egg rather than selling the golden egg for provisions. Sometimes churches do not grow because their members do not believe in sowing. *Sowing* is a biblical principle that teaches that we must sow into the lives and ministries of others if we expect to reap a harvest. Seed eaters are persons who believe that all collected contributions of the congregation are best spent on the congregation. These persons do not see the need to support associations, state conventions, or other benevolence ministries. When this type of thinking is predominant in a congregation, it produces an isolationist spirit. Yet, in many instances, the congregation never has enough funds to meet its needs in a timely fashion.

The Seed-eater Syndrome robs the congregation of its divine resources and creates a church culture of selfishness. The Bible teaches that our blessings come from giving. A non-giving congregation will not achieve its potential growth. Some small churches do not grow because they are constantly eating their harvest's seeds.

The Overflow Hater Syndrome

Within the *Overflow Hater Syndrome* is the overflow hater—a person who despises an overflow. This type of person would rather spend twenty-five dollars of thirty dollars rather than having thirty dollars and needing twenty-five dollars. The aim of this syndrome is to keep the church broke and, if not broke, then always on the financial begging list.

There are many reasons for the existence of this behavior among church members. Some members believe that a church is not to save money. Many of these persons have their reasons. Some church members believe that if the church's funds are not spent then they will be misappropriated—while others believe that the church is not a bank. Therefore, whatever future needs a congregation has can be resolved by passing the basket. This is known as the "basket mentality." It is a Sunday-to-Sunday financial plan for funding the ministries and expenses of a congregation. The problem with this type of funding is that it never allows the congregation to be proactive but, rather, causes it to be reactive in its mission and visions. Thus, some churches do not grow because they do not set aside funds to meet future developing and unexpected events.

Drama Queens and Kings

A *drama queen or king* is a person who operates in the negative. These types of persons are never satisfied. They live for the next rumor so that they may put their spin on it. They do not know how to be happy because they consistently live their lives under the wrong paradigm. These people do not use logic to navigate life's uncertainties but rather they are emotionally driven. They are like wolves covered in sheepskin, counting on the vulnerability of their next prey. They run and hang out with people who function in neutrality mode. They speak about a God of peace and love but they champion chaos and confusion. They have a destructive nature and only listen to their egos. They befriend people with smiles and tokenism for the purpose of future manipulative plots. They are dysfunctional sociopaths with multiple personalities. They are the "Jekylls and Hydes" of society. Some people see their good side, but most people will experience their dark side.

The purpose of the drama queen or king is to dethrone authority and replace it with a "me and I" syndrome. In other words, they seek to be the makers and shakers of an organization. In the church, if they cannot be the pastor's go-to person, then they will attack the pastor at every opportunity. Their goal is to diminish every gift within the congregational pew and limit it to their carnality.

The drama queen and king syndrome is a church killer. Unfortunately, too many small churches create a culture in which drama queens and kings can survive. Therefore, some small churches will never grow because they cultivate the environment for drama.

Even though church-killer tactics are visible, they are the afterbirth of fear. Fear is one of the primary reasons why smaller churches have little or no meaningful growth. If a congregation is to achieve its growth potential, then it must deal with fear wherever it appears.

Reflective and Critical Thinking

Discussion Questions:

- ❖ What practices do our congregations engage in that do more harm than good?

- ❖ What is our doctrine/process for including members in leadership roles?

- ❖ Does our congregation hold on to things that have no historical value that have outlived their usefulness?

- ❖ Does our congregation have a process that allows members to participate in the progression of the congregation that is transparent?

- ❖ Does our congregation have a process that allows members the opportunity to express grievances without being disruptive?

Chapter 3

Overcoming the Fear of Leadership

Being in leadership is not easy. It has its challenges. Even when God calls and appoints leaders, they will face resentment and disappointment.

Moses was called by God and appointed to lead Israel out of Egypt. Yet, he spent forty years being disliked and disappointed by a people he had been chosen to help. Ironically, there were moments when the people threatened to do him harm. Sometimes his challenges came from those who were related to him. Yet, facing immeasurable challenges, Moses did not allow fear to derail his assignment.

There are several characteristics of Moses' leadership style that, if followed, can help leaders overcome the challenge of fear. First, Moses was committed to his assignment. Commitment may not be appreciated by people, but it is honored by God.

Commitment is the pledging of oneself to undertake an assignment to its fruition. Thus, commitment acts as a shield against fear. Fear is the flooding or instability of one's emotions. Thus, unexpected, unappreciated, and threatening events are powerless against commitment.

Second, Moses was accountable to God. Where there is no accountability, there is a train wreck waiting to happen. One's knowing to whom he or she is accountable affords him or her the opportunity to minimize problems and visualize promises.

Accountability is the mental awareness of knowing to whom you are liable and answerable in all matters. In other words, accountability is the constitution for actions. Therefore, accountability governs one's actions and not the moment that requires an action. Thus, accountability is strengthened when faced with opposition. It prevents the person from being persuaded by other voices to do what would be counterproductive to his or her assignment. Thus, one's being accountable to God allows him or her to overcome fear. The Scripture challenges us not to be "eye servants"—only doing what we have been assigned to do when someone of human authority is watching us.

Third, Moses had an awareness of divine purpose. Moses did not seek to lead Israel according to his purpose; he led Israel with divine purpose. Moses' desire was not to establish his name but rather to make known the name of Jehovah. On several occasions, due to the disobedience of Israel, Moses had an opportunity to make his name greater than Abraham's, Isaac's, and Jacob's. Yet, he pleaded with God to honor the seed of Israel—not through his seed but of Abraham's. When a person leads with divine purpose, he or she will not seek to disconnect people from their history. Disconnecting people from their history, other than past sins, is leadership cloaked in fear.

Divine purpose can be best defined as obedience to God's agenda. Obedience to God's agenda gives leaders assurance in the midst of what appears to be defeat. This was true of the Hebrew boys and many other biblical patriarchs. God does not promise a life free of trials because we choose to obey Him. Yet, He does promise us that our trials will not defeat us.

Leadership undergirded in divine purpose encourages us to stay the course even when the course appears to be illogical. Leadership always performs best when its purpose is God's purpose. Imperfection is the greatest challenge that leaders face. However, divine purpose allows leaders to overcome imperfection because it reassures that it is "He" and not us that is performing.

Finally, divine purpose does not have a "see me" attitude. Jesus, in all of His glory, never did anything to uplift Himself. He came to do the will of the father.

Reflective and Critical Thinking

Discussion Questions:

- ❖ How can a congregation foster commitment among its membership?

- ❖ How can accountability of leadership improve the morale of our membership?

- ❖ Does our congregation see the need for accountability among its subordinate leaders?

- ❖ Is our congregation driven by divine purpose or twenty-first-century marketing techniques?

- ❖ Does our congregation's mission statement reflect biblical mandates?

Chapter 4

Turning Church Killers into Life Givers

Saul was a church killer until he met Christ on the Damascus Road. What did Christ see in Saul that Saul did not see in himself? It is Saul's Damascus Road experience that revealed his internal thoughts as they related to Jesus' personhood. Even though Saul persecuted the people of "the way," he must have had mixed feelings. His transformation reveals that he had had conflicting thoughts about the authenticity of Christ's message. In this revelatory moment, Saul could not dismiss Christ's claim of divinity. When a mysterious light shone on him, he asked a question: "Who are you, Lord?" Some people oppose change due to their lack of knowledge. Thus, the challenge becomes, how do we create moments that allow the Sauls of the twenty-first-century church to transform? In other words, how do we help congregants who employ church-killer tactics or who are traumatized by fear to become agents of life?

First, the pastor has to be free of fear and other leaders need to be in concert with the vision of the church to effectively defeat church-killer tactics. Just like hurricanes need warm water to remain powerful, those who use church-killer tactics require division among the membership in order to be effective. Admittedly, every person who uses church-killer tactics will not be converted. In other words, every congregation has an Agrippa—an *almost*-persuaded person.

Scripture reveals several important facts surrounding Saul's transformation: a personal crisis; his isolation from his cheerleaders; his direction to a place of healing; and a pronunciation of change in purpose. It has to be assumed that Saul was the only person in his group to look at the glow of the light. A sun flare is to be avoided at all costs, but for some reason Saul looked into the glare of the light. Is he like Moses, who saw something that defied natural logic? Whatever happened in that moment, two things occurred that did not happen to the others of the group. First, Saul was the only person to be blinded by the light. Second, Saul was the only person to hear Jesus' voice and to have a conversation with Him (see Acts 22:9).

God still has power to perform supernatural moments for His purpose. However, the church seems to be insensitive to God's work in the midst of those who are church killers. In order for human church killers to be transformed, they must be allowed to experience the supernatural moment without the carnal help of man.

Herein lies the challenge: man's sense of fairness often robs God of His opportunity to work in the human church killer's life.

> *A known disruptive member makes a mistake that demands a pastoral meeting, but on the day of the meeting some of the staff decide to invoke their sense of fairness.*

> *Thus, instead of the disruptive member seeking God for forgiveness and repentance, the disruptive member lives another day to cause confusion among the membership.*

Sometimes the supernatural moment is not pleasant. Yet, if member church killers are to be transformed, we must follow God's lead and not ask God to follow us. Church discipline can be an effective tool that helps church killers to seek God. The aim of church discipline is not to punish the violator but to help the violator to acknowledge Christ's sovereignty within the congregation's life. However, in Saul's case, it is Jesus Himself who called Saul's actions into account.

Saul had papers and instructions to go to Damascus to terrorize the church and not to be conciliatory with the church. Yet, no one in the group sought to stop him from experiencing the moment of blindness. It might be because they were truly concerned about his blindness. Whatever reason they had, they did not stop him from experiencing the supernatural moment. The moment started with blindness and ended with his sight being restored. However, between the starting and the ending, Saul fasted and repented. Church killers must be given space to communicate with God and repent before transformation can take place. Yet, most Christians fail to realize that asking for forgiveness and repentance are not the same. *Forgiveness* is the process of dismissing the mental effect of an unwanted and undesirable act—whereas *repentance* means one's changing his/her mind about an idea that causes the act for which an apology is required. Thus, for church killers to be transformed, they must be given time and space to seek God and repent.

So, to help twenty-first-century church killers, we must understand that they are spiritually blind. Persons who profess to be

Christians yet use church-killer tactics are spiritually blind. There is a difference between being spiritually blind and being demon-possessed. Often, the effect can be the same but the motive is different. They are both found in the congregation. The demon-possessed person opposes God and His authority—while the church killer is misguided and believes that he or she is working in the interest of God. Saul was a church killer; he was not demon-possessed. He truly believed that he was doing God a favor by persecuting the church. Thus, Saul was spiritually blind to God's prophetic truth.

Second, note that before healing and restoration could take place in Saul's life, God isolated him from his previous cohorts. Oftentimes, persons who are spiritually blind never complete the process of healing and restoration because they cannot divorce themselves from their corrupt past. Every idea, good or bad, has its cheerleaders. Thus, the spiritually blinded person needs to find a way to remove himself or herself from the cheerleaders of blindness. Many times, church killers never get the opportunity to be healed due to their so-called friends' intervention in the supernatural moment.

Saul was led to an anointed house to wait for an anointed person with a Rhema word. A *Rhema word* is a conversation that is tailor-made for the moment. The same methods exist today for those who are spiritually blind. The following are suggestions to aid the transformation of church killers:

- ➢ A house of worship that believes that God's world is relevant for twenty-first-century living.
- ➢ A pastor and church leaders whose lives are consistent with biblical truth.
- ➢ Attendance in Bible study and/or Sunday school.

> Acknowledgment and confession of sins.

> Seeking God's forgiveness and reestablishing a healthy prayer life.

Most people will not acknowledge their sins until they are convicted by the Word of God. Too often, Christians try to convince people that they are sinners or have committed an act of sin rather than sharing with them Christ's Word. Once we share the Word of God, and not our opinion, the Holy Spirit has an opportunity to convict the heart of a person.

Finally, notice that Saul's healing was not facilitated by someone that he knew but by someone he had the intent to harm. In other words, divine healing is often facilitated by the very person we seek to destroy or dislike. Therefore, those who are spiritually blinded in congregations might be asked to submit to the same pastor or church leader that they dislike for healing from God. Thus, the church killer has to be nourished by the understanding of the concept of submission. The restoration of sight demands submission as well as repentance. The healing of God cannot take place in the life of a spiritually blinded person until the opposition of God's appointed person has been resolved in the heart of the blinded person.

After Saul went to the appointed house, God sent a man to lay hands on Saul for the receiving of his physical sight. The receiving of Saul's (Paul's) sight was to enable him to fulfill the divine mission. In other words, God always equips us with tools to fulfill the ministry into which we are called. Thus, after a church killer has gone through a transformation moment, God will equip the church killer with tools to fulfill a divine mission.

In conclusion, church killers have kingdom-building skills, but their skills are misguided and misdirected. Like Jesus, the twenty-first-century church should strive to say "Lord, we have kept all of them that You gave, except the one." Yes, there will always be one that will refuse to change. However, an effective church is a church so structured that it makes it possible for church killers to become life givers.

Reflective and Critical Thinking

Discussion Questions:

- ❖ Why do people protect church killers?

- ❖ What does it mean to be fair as it relates to church discipline?

- ❖ Can you recall a Bible story that details how people were asked to look unto an object of harm for healing?

- ❖ Why is spiritual healing a necessity for church killers?

- ❖ Does our congregation have a process or procedures that can aid church killers to become life givers?

Chapter 5

Building the Team

Jesus and His disciples were a team. When Paul wrote to the Ephesians, he illustrated a team approach for defeating Satan's attacks. Church growth demands a team approach. A baseball player may have the ability to pitch a shut-out. Yet, in order to achieve his natural ability, it will require that he has a catcher of the same greatness.

In the sixth chapter of the book of Ephesians, Paul named several articles of clothing that are required for standing against the devil. He used the garments of a soldier as a comparative analysis for Christians to engage in spiritual warfare. He said that we need a belt, a breastplate, shoes, a shield, and a helmet. Paul was making the point that a soldier's success in a battle is not determined by faith and ability alone, but also by his or her willingness to be fully dressed for warfare. Therefore, church growth is not determined by faith alone, but by how well the members work as a team as well.

Using football as a model, a team has players, a coach, a general manager, and an owner. In congregations, we have players (members), a coach (Jesus Christ), a general manager (the Holy Spirit), and an owner (God the Father). In the game of football, the coach, general manager, and owner are persons of the flesh. In the church, the coach is Jesus Christ. The general manager is the Holy Spirit, and the owner is God, the Father. In a football game, every team has a quarterback. The purpose of the quarterback is to call the plays while in the game. In congregations, we have a quarterback—the pastor. However, unlike the game of football, the game never ends for the pastor.

In the game of football, the quarterback is to call the plays and team members are to execute the called plays according to their assigned positions. In the game of football, there are two positions that can determine the outcome of a game: defense and offense.

The offensive tacklers protect the quarterback from the tackling of the opposing team. In other words, the offensive tacklers allow the quarterback time to execute the called play. The defensive tacklers protect the quarterback gains by preventing the opposition from moving the ball down the field. In the congregation, the offensive tacklers are the deacons or stewards. They are to protect the pastor from opposition. All church leaders, ministries, and members are players. These persons and ministries have been assigned positions to make gains for kingdom building and to make sure that Satan does not take back gained yardage. In other words, as a congregation makes gains, Satan will seek to take back lost territory.

Growing congregations understand the paradigm of the football team's structure. The owner of the team has the resources to purchase the team but does not manage the team. The manager has knowledge of the team's structure but does not coach the team. The coach has one job: to produce a winning team. In other words, the coach has to know the game and help guide the players into achieving their best while in the game. This is why Paul admonished the church not to call novices as church leaders.

When the game starts, the most important person at the game is the coach, and the most important persons in the game are the quarterback and players. Likewise, the most important person in the congregation is the Holy Spirit, and the most important position in the church is the pastor/bishop. Too many smaller congregations fail to see the biblical importance of a pastor. In this sense, they are like Orthodox Israelites who acknowledge God but reject the Son of God. The pastor is not the coach, but he has been assigned by the Coach to call the plays.

While there are similarities between a congregation and a football team, there are major differences in their application and purpose. The football team's purpose is to perform at a level that secures the investment of the owner and continues to make money for the franchise. However, the purpose of the congregation is to win souls for the kingdom of God and to be the agency that proclaims the Good News of Jesus Christ. Yet, this cannot be accomplished effectively without a team approach.

When building a team within a congregation, a congregation should engage in close scrutiny of these positions: the elders, stewards or deacons, support personnel, trustees, music ministry, ushers and/or greeters, and other key ministries of the congregation. In some congregations, there is a board of elders that works with the pastor and even has authority to change or redirect pastoral leadership. Also, in many Baptist churches there is an "Official Board." The Official Board, based upon the language of the church's by-laws, has the authority to act without consent of the membership and, in some instances, has the power to derail pastoral visionary leadership.

Therefore, it is imperative that attention be paid to and prayer be lifted up for key positions in the congregation. In other words, you want people in key positions who believe that their position is secondary to the growth of the congregation.

If a congregation is to grow to its potential, it must move beyond the fear of team building. Team building is a process that allows and recognizes the unique gifts of others to function as collaborative enablers to achieve a desired goal. In order for the process to be effective, it demands mutual respect and an understanding of the roles and responsibilities of each team member.

First, team building demands that a clear, definitive goal be articulated by the pastor/bishop. However, it does not need to be the express idea of the pastor/bishop to be a goal of the congregation. Too many pastors/bishops make the mistake of not implementing things because it did not come forth from their mouths initially.

> *For instance, the church is seeking a time to worship and one of the team members suggests a time to meet. Does the leader not consider it because it wasn't the leader's idea?*

Effective pastors/bishops must see themselves as enablers of ideas and not the sole creators of ideas. This is not to say that pastors/bishops are not expected to bring ideas to a team, but it is to say that not all worthwhile ideas come only from the pastor/bishop.

Few pastors are called to an assignment that has a working staff. Most pastors are called to an assignment where they are expected to be the water boy and batboy. Yet, the pastor cannot do everything if the congregation is to achieve its growth potential. Thus, the dilemma is, how do you bring others into the mix to create a team?

In some instances, persons will recognize genuine leadership and seek to be members of a team. However, most people are members of a team because they were discovered to have the skills needed for the team. Thus, every good coach knows what skills are needed in order to afford a team the possibility of a win. Perhaps this is why some congregations require their members to take a spiritual-gifts test before being assigned to a leadership position. Jesus knows the gifts that each of us has. Therefore, picking team members will require observation. It is better to choose persons that have a skill instead of taking a chance that a person will become what is desired.

Even though a person may have a desired skill, it is important to remember that even the best of us are flawed. The newspapers have a myriad of stories of persons who processed a skill to get them on a team but were dismissed from the team because of flawed character. Thus, a secret to team building for congregations is to know how and with whom to share authority, and having a system that holds persons accountable for their actions. This would require that a person's assignment be delineated in writing. When sharing authority with a person, a person does not need to *guess* what he or she has been authorized to do—that person needs to *know*.

Most small congregations frown upon putting things in writing, but having things in writing can prevent things from getting out of hand. People need to know their duties and responsibilities and the consequences of their not fulfilling their obligations. The size of a congregation has nothing to do with whether or not a congregation should have written duties for its staff and subordinated leaders.

For most pastors, it is a struggle to build a team ministry. However, if a congregation wants to maximize its potential to win souls for God's kingdom, then a team ministry can greatly facilitate the goal.

And if subordinated leaders want to maximize their participation for God's kingdom, they will welcome a team ministry. A team ministry gives the Holy Spirit the opportunity to utilize spiritual gifts and talents within a given congregation. Therefore, it is very important that the pastor assign value to each position on the team. Also, it is important that each person master his/her position on the team and respect the pastor. A team that has respect for each position and each person on the team can have strategic meetings without conflict.

Finally, a team ministry is effective when the goal is clearly articulated and members of the team are in agreement with the goal to be achieved. When articulating a goal, try to create an acronym. For instance, Second Missionary Baptist Church's goal is "W.E.E.M"— which stands for Worship, Evangelism, Education, and Mission. The goal is not the method but it is the aim. Now, *methodology* is a process of achieving the goal and may vary according to different auxiliaries and departments within a given congregation. Thus, do not make the mistake of trying to achieve unity in methodology. Methodology is always determined by the objective of the goal. In other words, goals need definitive objectives.

In conclusion, kingdom building is a team-ministry effort and not a solo performance. After the 9/11 attack by operatives of Osama bin Laden upon Americans, the federal government realized that its agencies were not communicating with each other in a manner that maximized protection for Americans. In the same vein, many churches are not maximizing their potential because auxiliaries and departments do not work together and share information that is vital for healthy church growth. Team ministry is not an "I" but a "we" concept. It is the manner in which Jesus Christ chose to build His kingdom.

Finally, there is erosion and slow death of local district associations and state and national conventions due to the lack or unwillingness of congregations to be team players. Congregations are more than just gatherers to social meetings, choir recitals, Bible study, and morning worship. Each congregation is comprised of team members of the body of Christ. Thus, each congregation is challenged to maximize its potential to share Jesus Christ's teachings by joining with others in a manner that serves to add new souls to Christ's kingdom.

Reflective and Critical Thinking

Discussion Questions:

- ❖ What does a qualified pastor need to grow a church ministry?

- ❖ Why is it important for church members to know their position as it relates to church growth?

- ❖ Who has God positioned in the church to call the plays for church growth?

- ❖ Would the general manager of a football team give a play to a player to execute in a game without telling the quarterback?

- ❖ So, why would the Holy Spirit tell a member to exercise a ministry strategy without telling the pastor?

- ❖ What is the difference between a goal and methodology?

Chapter 6

A Paradigm for Church Growth

A *paradigm* is a model that tells you where you need to start and what you need to do to get to where you want to go. However, a church model for growth starts with the philosophy of "understanding" and commitment to the mission of Jesus Christ's church.

It appears that many are abandoning the mission of Christ's church for twenty-first-century marketing techniques. Christ's church is more than a large building, large crowds, and a choreographed worship moment. Now, God is not against a large building, crowds, or a dramatic presentation in the worship moment. Yet, meaningful church growth is a process that seeks to win souls for God's kingdom while providing the opportunity for transformation. Thus, the foundation of church growth is based in the natural and spiritual. It is natural in the sense that every congregation that grows has mothers who give birth to the congregation. It is spiritual in the sense that congregations participate in the regeneration process by identifying new converts for a Holy Spirit encounter.

Step #1: The Philosophy of Understanding

The apostle Paul admonished the Roman converts to be transformed and not to conform to the world (see Romans 12:2). Thus, the objective of divine and meaningful church growth is not for the sake of a building, crowds, or presentation. Therefore, the philosophy of "understanding" must be utilized for effective church growth.

The Bible admonishes us to get understanding in all that we do (see Proverbs 4:7). There is a reason for getting understanding. If the fear of God is the beginning of wisdom, then the knowledge of God is understanding. In other words, to know God is to understand God. The ultimate objective of a congregation is to assist God as an agent of transformation. In other words, the church is an institution of salvation and sanctification. The church is the light of the world (see Matthew 5:14). Just as nature is transformed and harnessed to provide light for the natural eye, so people are to be transformed by the Word of God in order to provide light for the spiritual eye as well as the natural eye. This process takes place in the church: the body of Christ. However, the body of Christ gathers in buildings which we call churches, houses of prayer, or worship centers. Thus, the question is, "How does the physical institution best represent God as it seeks to participate in divine growth?" Now, physical institutions can increase their populations without being true to God's agenda. Thus, the increase in population within a physical institution is not necessarily church growth. Sometimes growth is a swelling, and anything that swells is infected. Therefore, divine church growth has to be rooted in the philosophy of understanding who God is.

It is understanding that allows us the opportunity to know God's commandments. "Your hands have made and fashioned me; Give me understanding, that I may learn Your commandments" (Psalm 119:73,

NKJV). In other words, our relying upon our own understanding is counterproductive to divine church growth. God has commandments that facilitate growth. Failing to adhere to God's commandments produces growth stagnation; it encourages unchanged people to attend an institution of change without the possibility of spiritual growth. Thus, church growth is not predicated upon the number of people who join in the worship moment but upon the number of people who undergo spiritual transformation.

> *For an example, church "A" has one hundred people attending worship. They go to church acting like sinners and they leave church acting like sinners. On the other hand, church "B" has twenty-five people attending worship. They go to church acting like sinners but they leave church acting like Christ. The world sees church A as church growth, but God sees church B as church growth.*

The difference is that church "A" introduced the people to theatrics, whereas church "B" introduced the people to God's commandments and precepts. Understanding who God is and what He desires helps us to enable people in the worship moment. It gives worshippers the opportunity to grow spiritually. When we have understanding, we realize that God's testimonies are more important than our testimony (see Psalm 119:125; Matthew 28:20).

In the business world, people sometimes will say to a friend or acquaintance, "I can get you in the room but your talents must keep you in the room." Preachers have a saying: "Your gift will make room for you." In other words, what gains you access may not be what sustains you. The Proverbs writer said, "Through wisdom a house is built, And by understanding it is established" (Proverbs 24:3, NKJV). Many of us have witnessed major franchises go broke and mega-churches close their doors. The book of Proverbs helps us to know that having understanding is just as important as having wisdom. In other words, knowing how to keep the building standing is just as important as knowing how to build a building. The implication is, "It's one thing to take a horse to the water trough, but it is another thing to teach a horse to return to the water trough."

Finally, understanding allows the believer to draw from the well of God's counseling (see Proverbs 20:5). God has deposited His counseling into the heart of every believer. It is our understanding of Him that enables us to draw from His fountain. Without the aid of God's counseling, the life of the believer is aimless. Therefore, the first step for church growth starts with the "philosophy of understanding." Thus, the church, house of prayer, or worship center cannot grow divinely without first having an understanding of who God is.

Step #2: Know What You Want

It is very important to know what you want before you receive it. Knowing what you want is more than the aesthetic of a desire. Knowing what you want is an inclusive thought that encompasses responsibilities, purpose, and oppositions of a desired object or position. Thus, the Bible states, "If a man desires the office of bishop, he desires a good thing" (see 1 Timothy 3:1). Therefore, the text implies that the position is good because of what it demands of the seekers. Consequently, those who are willing to sacrifice self for God's kingdom are pleasing in His sight. The pastor has to know what is desired before stepping into the role of overseer.

While leadership must stem from the pastor, the pastor cannot grow the congregation alone. There is a saying among pastors and preachers that "sheep beget sheep." While this is a true statement, it is the shepherd's voice that a sheep hears. In other words, it is the shepherd's job to provide a spiritual diet that causes sheep to multiply. One's knowing what he or she wants before he or she gets it allows him or her the opportunity to maximize potentiality. Furthermore, this prepares one for future distractions. Wanting something but not knowing why you want it is a recipe for disappointment. This is perhaps the leading cause for leadership dysfunction within a church's auxiliaries and departments.

Step #3: Choose a Team

The success of church growth will require you to choose persons for your team. In most instances, persons will have been assigned to auxiliaries and departments before your arrival. Therefore, it is important to ask for any information that an auxiliary or department has in progress. Take time to analyze information before dismissing any previous initiatives. And if previous methods and objectives are too deficient to achieve the goal of the ministry, take time to explain it to the group or congregation. Do not get mired down in trying to change things but seek to add new life and direction for the congregation. Finally, make sure that whatever you do is necessary.

Sometimes, a pastor will receive an assignment where the congregation is organized and has by-laws. In these instances, the congregation expects the pastor to function as a Pastor/C.E.O. In other words, they do not expect the pastor to micro-manage. In this instance, the pastor is expected to bring the staff together to see if they are meeting stated goals and objectives. If goals are not being met, then the pastor is expected to give leadership that will allow stated objectives to be achieved. Effective pastoral leadership gives life and new direction to stated objectives that are relevant and true to the mission of Christ's church. To achieve desired objectives might necessitate a change in subordinated leadership or modification of methodology. Whatever the pastor does, it has to be done in accordance with the congregational by-laws. Not understanding and knowing how to navigate the church's by-laws is a recipe for chaos. Too many young pastors have difficulty with creative leadership when being called to churches that have written by-laws. Changing something is not leadership but leadership will effect change.

There are times when a pastor receives an assignment and there are not any church's by-laws and no meaningful structure for growth. In this instance, the pastor has to multiply himself to achieve desired church growth. This is Jesus' model. Jesus multiplied Himself. It is Andrew who recognized Jesus as the possible Messiah. This means that Christ conducted Himself in a Messianic mode.

When a pastor is assigned to a ministry that is without meaningful structure and members, the pastor's genuine love for God and the people of God dictates the possibility for growth. Most pastors fail to study and understand Jesus' model for growth:

- He lived a lifestyle that attracted faith seekers.
- He understood His mission objectives.
- He was steadfast in His convictions.
- He chose busy people.
- He instructed His disciples.

- He showed His disciples examples of His teaching.

- He sent His disciples into the mission field.

- He corrected His disciples.

- He loved His disciples unconditionally.

The above list is subjective and does not list all that can be learned of Christ's methodology for church growth. Yet, it does allow one to see some key elements for church growth. It also exposes many weaknesses as it relates to church growth.

Every congregation has a seed for growth. A small congregation may have some difficult members but it has a seed for growth. In this instance, the leader has to attract the seed. Leaders have to demonstrate seed knowledge before a seed submits to the planting of a new vision.

Christ understood His mission objective. Understanding a mission objective includes being obedient to the mission sender. Thus, Mark's gospel reads, "For even the Son of man came not to be ministered unto, but to minister, and to give his life a ransom for many" (Mark 10:45). Therefore, it is imperative for every leader to know his/her mission objective in order to effectuate congregational growth.

Not only did Christ understand His mission objective but also He was steadfast in His conviction. One's being steadfast in his or her convictions shields that person from distractions. Yet, conviction is not an excuse for having a go-alone attitude. Conviction is an assurance that the outcome of a goal is worthy of the investment into a goal—which is another way of saying that methodology is not conviction but a means of achieving the outcome of a goal.

If the outcome of a goal is worthy of conviction, then choosing the right person to participate in the process is imperative. Often, church growth is hindered by placing the wrong person on the team. This is especially true in smaller congregations. With the exception of Judas Iscariot, Christ's chosen disciples were devoted and committed followers. Finally, Christ chose persons who were industrious.

I had an opportunity to meet the late Adrian Rogers, pastor of Bellevue Baptist Church of Memphis, Tennessee. He said to us, "Every person that joined Bellevue was trained [in] how Bellevue functioned regardless of who they were or where they came from." In other words, before a person could be on Bellevue's team he or she was taught by the pastor. Christ taught His disciples. Churches that grow take time to teach their team members. An untrained congregation may swell, but it will never grow.

> *A young pastor was seeking to become the pastor of a larger congregation. He was impressed with how the finance committee functioned. He was very impressed with their Sunday tithing. However, he never asked the church about its commitment to training. His belief was if the church knows how to record and track its funds and they have funds on hand, he could do ministry.*

Unfortunately, this is the mindset of too many pastors. They elevate money over training.

Finally, the spiritual growth as well as numerical growth of a congregation are tied to its training initiatives and not to its Sunday morning tithes. Effective and sustainable ministry is the fruit of infectious and purpose-driven training. Christ taught His disciples.

While Christ taught His disciples, He was not afraid to correct them. Correction is an act of love. The Bible teaches that God chastens those whom He loves. Yet, because of fear, too often many leaders never point out the errors of those whom they lead. When uncorrected errors go without correction, it produces division and insubordination.

Step #4: Honor Other People's Journey

Give honor to other people's journey. As a leader, look for and magnify the good of those who are followers. It is natural for us to desire validation. Often the people to whom God gives us opportunity to lead have been followers of another leader. Validating people's pasts gives them a freedom to move forward. In other words, do not use your opportunity to lead to crucify those who have gone before you.

Too many leaders waste time comparing themselves to their predecessors. Every leader has to lead in their season. Therefore, planting is different from cultivating. Cultivating is different from harvesting. The objective of leadership is to know which season you are in during your assignment.

Step #5: Articulate the Vision

People cannot read your mind. Therefore, the vision has to be articulated. Sometimes leaders fail to clearly articulate the vision for growth. It is difficult for people to follow a vision if it is not consistent or is poorly presented. A vision for growth involves more than statements. A growth vision has to be undergirded with direction, assignments, and a plan for implementation. Furthermore, a growth vision needs to be reliable and steady. Thus, a church-growth vision needs to be trustworthy and biblically sound.

Step #6: Face the Fear of Your Vision

Nothing in life is without challenges. Therefore, every leader has to face the fear of his or her vision. Leadership is an opportunity for fear. In other words, fear exists for the sole purpose of hindering mobility. Even when fear works on the behalf of one's betterment, it hinders mobility. For instance, a child learns to fear the heat of flames. Thus, the fear of flames hinders the child from exercising his or her curiosity. Fear is the reason why most planning sessions end up being nothing more than selective social gatherings.

A vision that is not implemented is a daydream at the expense of mental potentiality. Once a vision has been articulated, it has to be implemented. Thus, fear will work overtime to hinder the mobility of one's vision. Therefore, face the naysayers and doubters. If the vision has been undergirded biblically and wisely, the then voice of naysayers and doubters is indication of its value and authenticity. Finally, plan a launching date for every new vision in order to maximize its impact.

Step #7: Implementation of the Vision

The seventh step is the implementation of a vision. Implementation demands trust in God, logistics, and methodology. The Bible teaches that one is not to lean unto his or her own understanding. Thus, no amount of planning will guarantee the success of a vision. Therefore, it is imperative to place trust in God for the success of a vision—the reason being that a vision ought to be a reflection of God's will for kingdom building. When a vision reflects God's will and people operate in the integrity of God's will, success is assured.

Many visions do not achieve their natural potential or spiritual impact due to poor logistical deliveries. In order words, the distribution of the vision's ideas and goals are not sufficient. For example, the vision of the locomotive was a brilliant idea, but without railroad tracks it would not have achieved its potential. Therefore, every vision requires logistical preparation to achieve its potential.

Listed are some factors that need to be considered for the implementation of a vision:

- ✓ Where will the vision's initiatives take place?
- ✓ Who will it impact?
- ✓ How many people are needed to carry out the vision's initiatives?
- ✓ What physical facility will be needed to house and/or present the vision's initiatives?
- ✓ What positions will be needed for coordination of the vision's goals?
- ✓ What expenses will be incurred to implement the vision's initiatives?
- ✓ Does the vison's initiative meet current needs?
- ✓ Is the delivery of the vision's initiative accessible to those whom it will impact?

Just as important as logistical preparedness is to the success of a vision, so is methodology. Whereas logistical preparedness deals with "who, what, where, etc.," methodology answers the question that deals with "how." How something is done is a process. The vision's initiatives are not birthed into existence. Therefore, methods will be required in order to implement the vision's initiatives. Also, methods will vary depending upon positions to achieve the goals of the visions. Thus, the methodology is determined by the vision's initiative. When the concept is applied to a congregation, it is possible and practical for each auxiliary to have different methods to achieve church growth. In addition, methods will need to be modified in order to stay relevant to the intent of the vision's initiative. The absence of relevancy is the demise of many good visions.

Salvation of lost souls ought to be an external vision of every Christian church. The winning of souls is an act of evangelism. In the 1960s, most churches held a week of revival to win souls for Christ's church. Yet, in the twenty-first century, revivals are not held to win souls as much as they are held to revive saved souls. Therefore, methods to win souls vary according to time. For example, when I was a boy, I did not have an iPad or Smart phone on which to study the Bible. Yet, iPads and Smart phones are tools that can be utilized for Bible study and the sharing of God's Word to the unsaved of our communities. Thus, it would be foolish not to use these tools as a means of achieving the goal of evangelism.

Smart phones and iPads are tools that can be used for church school and Bible study. In addition, many congregations are now using Facetime, Skype, and live streaming to replace the traditional teaching moments in the church's life. Refusing not to use these tools because they were not available in the apostles' days is foolish and without scriptural insight.

In conclusion, there are some things that grow a congregation. On the other hand, there are some things that swell a congregation—such as a music ministry—without the preaching and teaching of the Gospel's concepts and precepts. Therefore, it ought to be every congregation's desire to grow, not swell. There is no substitute for doctrinal preaching, teaching, and Holy Ghost-inspired praise for church growth. Methodology and logistical needs may change, but the Word of God remains the same throughout generations.

There is no magical moment or event that will grow a congregation such as building a new sanctuary, starting a media ministry, having gospel concerts, or inviting famous people to speak on special days. These things may take place in certain congregations but they within themselves do not grow a congregation. Therefore, do not waste your time attempting to do what others are doing. Imitation without preparation is like driving the wrong way on a busy street. Stop hating, do what Jesus did, and your congregation will grow.

A Paradigm for Church Growth

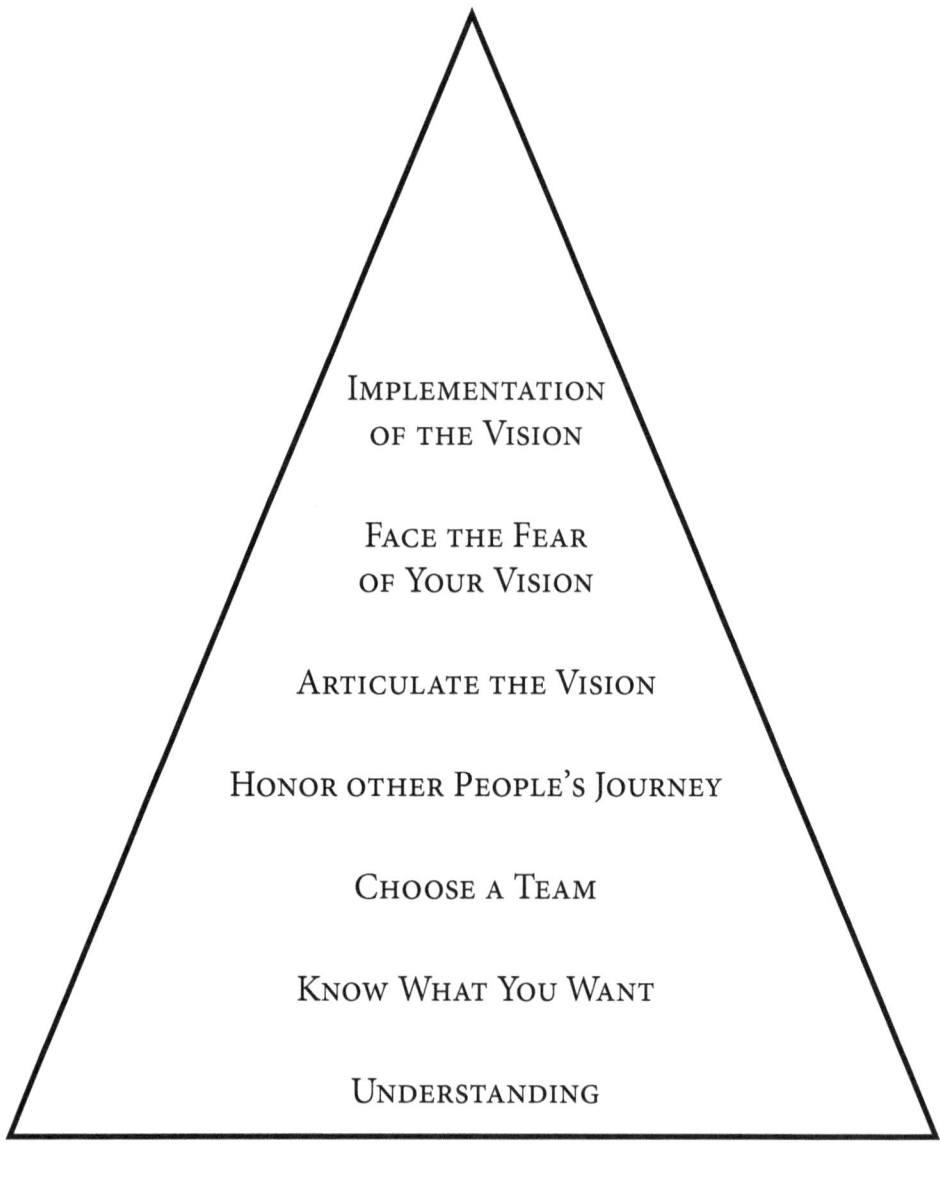

Reflective and Critical Thinking

Discussion Questions:

- ❖ Why is understanding who God is crucial in order for church growth to take place?

- ❖ Why is it important to know all of the details of what you want before receiving it?

- ❖ What is the relationship between the validation of past accomplishments and the future growth of a congregation?

- ❖ What is the difference between logistical preparedness and methodology?

- ❖ What is the one thing that can cause the demise of a realized vision?

Chapter

When Fear Stagnates Church Growth

In this chapter, we seek to give a summary and answer to the question of what happens when fear stagnates church growth. When we allow fear to stagnate the church's growth, we become little "Adams and Eves"—giving to the devil what belongs to God. Often, the story of Adam and Eve is viewed through the lens of male and female or husband and wife. However, the story is really about the consequences of fear. It is fear that propelled Eve to believe that God was intentionally withholding valuable information from her. Most of the time we view fear as that emotion that causes us to seek shelter or to run, but sometimes fear causes us to act inappropriately and unwisely. Eve's insecurity led her to distrust the Creator and to involve her husband in an act of disobedience.

Fear is antithetical to trust. The aim of intrusive fear is to disarm and disconnect one from reality. When one is disconnected from reality, disobedience becomes a norm and not an anomaly. Disobedience leads to growth stagnation.

When we allow fear to stagnate church growth, we become a people hoping for a manifestation while rejecting its reality. This is why the Hebrews of the Jewish faith rejected Christ. The Jewish faith of Jesus' era failed to grow because of a disconnection between hope and realization. Hope has an end—it is called *realization*. Yet, there are times when a congregation fails to grow because of hopeless hope. *Hopeless hope* is one's inability or refusal to take possession of the fruit of that which is hoped for. (Hopeless hope is like a child hoping for a basketball and the father placing a basketball in his or her hands and him or her refusing to dribble the ball.) Sometimes, fear creates a stagnation that produces a disposition of hopeless hope.

Stagnation produces procrastination. Procrastination is the enemy of opportunity. Many congregations have missed opportunities to grow due to procrastination. Sometimes we put things off due to fear.

Stagnation sometimes causes one to be indecisive. Indecisiveness is a by-product of fear. Indecisiveness is a protester of intentionality. A person who is indecisive is afraid of making the wrong choice. Sometimes, the fear of making the wrong choice is a lack of preparation for the moment. However, there are times when the fear of making the wrong choice is tied to the effect of the choice. In other words, will the decision cause retaliation or failure?

Finally, stagnation leads to decay. When a living thing or person starts decaying, it is a sign of death. In other words, a stagnated congregation is a dying congregation. A dying congregation will not attract people who are seeking life. Thus, every congregation that seeks to attract new members has to be growth-minded.

As one can see, fear produces stagnation and stagnation has a myriad of side effects that hinder church growth. Yet, the aim of this book is not to focus on fear but to identify it and control its effect. Thus, whether you are a pilot or stewardess, your duty is to operate toward the end of the safety of the passengers. Likewise, whether you are the usher or pastor, your duty is to help facilitate the growth of God's kingdom.

In summary, every congregation is to be a growing congregation. If a congregation is not adding new members, it is a sign of decay. When there is evidence of decay, the leadership needs to perform a biopsy in order to determine the cause of decay. Furthermore, congregations need to protect themselves from becoming an environment for drama. Serious-minded people do not prefer to be part of a scandalous congregation. If and when a congregation adds people in the midst of continual and outrageous scandals, it is an indication that spiritual growth has been abandoned for an infectious swelling.

In every congregation, there will be members who challenge leadership. Sometimes, it will be due to a lack of understanding. However, there will be persons who challenge the leadership's decisions for no other reason than to cause chaos. As Christ's parable teaches, we are to make attempts to save the lost. Sometimes people are like animals—they get lost. Some people are lost to reality or lost due to pain and suffering. Thus, it is our responsibility to make an attempt to turn church killers into life givers.

Leadership is an opportunity for fear. Fear is a master at disguising itself. Sometimes it will masquerade as protector. At other times, fear can produce a humble and meek spirit. While we are to have humble and meek spirits, when it is the by-product of fear, it leads to passivity. Therefore, every leader—whether the pastor or church's secretary—must face fear and defeat it.

Choosing a team is paramount to success and church growth. Having a good team allows the pastor or a subordinated leader the opportunity to share authority without the fear of compromising pulpit or positional authority. However, if given the opportunity to choose team members, do not choose unteachable, unqualified, or uncommitted persons.

In conclusion, make sure that goals are clearly defined. A team member should never have to guess what his or her responsibility is to the team. Therefore, it is always best to have written duties and responsibilities for each team member's assignment. Finally, be a good listener and learn how to implement the ideas of team members, especially when the ideas are consistent with the desired objectives of the congregation.

Reflective and Critical Thinking

Discussion Questions:

❖ Can you see fear as being a factor in Eve and Adam's disobedience?

❖ Can you identify instances in your life or the church's life when fear disconnected you from reality?

❖ Is there something that you know that you need to do but have not done? Ask yourself what the cause of your procrastination is.

❖ Why should one be concerned about numerical growth in a congregation in the midst of serious and continuous scandals?

❖ Why is choosing a good team paramount for success even when the leader is qualified for the position?

Appendices

A. GLOSSARY OF TERMINOLOGY

- **Cannibalization:** a term used among church data professionals to describe the growth of giga-churches that feed off of smaller mega-churches.

- **Commitment:** the pledging of oneself to undertake an assignment to its fruition.

- **Controller Syndrome:** a dictatorial managerial style employed by a person to limit the input and assessment of a specified task by other persons within a defined group of people.

- **Doctrine of Inclusivity:** a method that seeks to include everybody in participation of something within a defined group of persons.

- **Fear:** the flooding of or instability of one's emotions.

- **Fishing-hole Syndrome:** defined as the belief that making superficial changes that imitates others will produce like results.

- **Giga-church:** a congregation that has ten thousand or more members who attend worship regularly each week.

- **Hopeless Hope:** when one is unable or refuses to take possession of the fruit of that which is hoped for.

- **Isolationism:** defined as an attitude of exclusivism that does not see the benefits of participating in a larger community.

- **Jeroboam Syndrome:** a disorder held by leadership that casts itself as having concern for others but in actuality is predicated upon fear.

- **Logistical Lies:** untruths told for the sole purposes of maintaining a position.

- **Logistical Outpost:** defined as where things take place and by whom, and under what condition they take place.

- **Mega-church:** a congregation that has two thousand or more members who attend worship regularly each week.

- **Methodology:** the study of methods. Methods deal with how to perform an act.

- **Non-committal Leadership:** a style of leadership whereby the leader is disconnected from reality.

- **Overflow Hater Syndrome:** a disorder held by a person or persons that do not want to see the congregation with extra funds. These are usually people who do not believe that the church should have a savings account or investments. They believe that the church should operate Sunday to Sunday.

- **Passive Leadership:** a style of leadership whereas the leader is acted upon rather than creating acts that impact the congregational life positively.

- **Pulpit Authority:** the right and power entrusted only into the hands of the pastor/bishop of the church.

- **Resistance Syndrome:** a push-back tactic.

- **Rhema word:** a phrase describing a word or phrase that speaks to the matter at hand.

- **Seed-eater Syndrome:** when there is a desire to spend all of the congregation's collected funds on the congregation and not to sow funds into other worthy causes and ministries. Congregations that hold to this concept usually do not give to collaborative efforts of associations and conventions, or have a strong internal mission initiative.

- **Shark-minded:** vicious and territorial.

- **Small-vision Syndrome:** when one sees oneself as insignificant or not able to achieve a given assignment or goal. People of this mindset always magnify the problems more than the promises of God.

- **Status Seekers:** persons who join a congregation of notoriety for the purpose of boosting their personal status among their peers.

- **Traditions:** sentiments or established norms of the past that are tied to ideology or methodology. (However, there are some biblical practices that are labeled as traditions that should never be abandoned.)

- **Unchurched:** a term used primarily to refer to persons who have accepted Jesus Christ, but are not faithful to a particular congregation. However, in some instances, persons of this category may not be attending a church.

- **Undermining Syndrome:** a tactic used to produce failure.

- **Unhealthy Sentiments:** strong feelings that hold a congregation to its past at the price of being unproductive.

B. TWELVE THINGS THAT HINDER CHURCH GROWTH

- Unprepared or untrainable leaders
- Unrealistic expectations
- An unclear vision of the mission
- Failure to implement discussed and approved policies
- An abandonment of discipleship training for ministry's initiatives
- A soloist attitude
- Archaic methodologies
- An inability or unwillingness to hold people accountable
- An unappreciative ideology for a team concept
- An unwillingness or inability to share authority
- An unhealthy and non-productive relationship with the past
- A failure to promote the theology of Christ and the practicality of His teachings

C. A CHURCH DEMOGRAPHIC SURVEY

A demographic survey can help a congregation to develop meaningful ministries. Too often, ministries in congregations do not reflect the needs of the membership or community that they serve. To get the best participation, do not ask people to include their name on the survey.

Question #1: What is your age? 18-25; 26-35; 36-45; 46-55; 56-65; 66-76; 77 and over

Question #2: What is your gender? Male ____ Female ____

Question #3: What is your relationship status? Married; Single; Divorced; Widow; Widower

Question #4: How many children are living in your home under 12 years of age? ____; 18 years of age? ____ 35 years of age? ____

Question #5: How many grandchildren or great-grandchildren are you the primary caregiver for? ____

Question #6: Do you own private transportation? Yes ____ No ____

Question #7: What is your occupation status? Employed; Semi-employed; Self-employed; Retired; Disabled

Question #8: Do you receive any federal assistance other than social security or veteran payments? Yes ____ No ____

Question #9: Are you a veteran? Yes ____ No ____

Question #10: Do you have a job that involves travel outside of the city or relocation possibility? Yes ___ No ___

Question #11: What is your educational status? College ___; Graduate School ___; High School or Equivalent ___

Question #12: What is your housing status? Homeowner ___; Renter ___

Question #13: What is the zip code of your dwelling? _____

Question #14: How many years have you been a Christian? 50 years or more; 40 years or more; 30 years or more; 20 years or more; 10 years or less

Question #15: Of what church auxiliary are you a member? Women; Men; Youth; Children; Senior; Young Adult; Usher/Greeter; Education; Choir; None; Other _____

Question #16: Have you recently attended a church workshop, association, or convention in the Christian Education Congress? Yes ___ No ___

Question #17: Have you recently shared your Christian faith with a friend, family member, or neighbor? Yes ___ No ___

Question #18: Do you know of persons or families that need some personal assistance with some household needs? Yes ___ No ___

Question #19: Do you know any children who need tutorial help? Yes ___ No ___

Question #20: Are you willing to volunteer for church's needs based upon your skill level? Yes ___ No ___ Maybe ___

Question #21: What are some of your skills? Lawn care; Electrical; Plumbing; Culinary; Educational; Legal; Finance; Other(s) _____

Question #22: Are you a business owner? Yes ___ No ___

Question #23: Are you a manager with hiring responsibilities? Yes ___ No ___

Question #24: Are you in a law-enforcement occupation? Yes ___ No ___

Question #25: Are you a teacher? Elementary ___ High school ___ College ___ Other _____

D. CHURCH MYTHS THAT HINDER CHURCH GROWTH

- The church is a volunteer organization.
- The church has to manipulate members to honor stewardship.
- You cannot expect or demand commitment of church members.
- Evangelism is more important than discipleship or vice versa.
- Programs take precedence over purpose.
- The 80-20 rule is the average for church operation and participation.
- Church attendance is not important.

E. FIVE PRINCIPLES OF THE GREAT COMMISSION

- ✓ Evangelism
- ✓ Discipleship training
- ✓ Fellowship time
- ✓ Ministry availability
- ✓ Worship time

F. A PERSONAL OBSERVATION OF CHURCH TRENDS

Congregations that have less than two hundred active and supporting members may be out of business in the next twenty-five years. They are on the endangered church list according to some churches' statisticians. If their doors aren't closed, they will be irrelevant. The irrelevancy will have nothing to do with the message but the practicality and application of the message for a digital society. A digital society will not be attractive to archaic methodologies and regressive delivery platforms. Generation "D" children will be digital-minded. They will usher in digital worship as a norm. Many of them will attend churches where the preacher is telecasted to the congregation.

How we communicate impacts our worship habits and practices. Therefore, Generation "D" children will have a different reason for assembly and what takes place in the moment of the assembly. People of a digital generation will seek a message that is true and practical. In other words, if you preach a God that provides, and your place of worship is outdated for human comfort, technologically deficient, and sustainability inept, it will be an indictment of belief and application. In the next twenty-five years, churches that are not equipped to deal with the basic needs of its members will be viewed as operating without divine license and guilty of theological malpractice.

The Mom-and-Pop houses of worship are fading fast from the fabric of the Christian community. Most of these congregations are located in rural communities or in the storefronts of cities. A *Mom-and-*

Pop house of worship is defined as a congregation with a membership of less than twenty-five members. Also, the family churches will see a decline. A *family church* is a church that was started by one or more families. These types of congregations are primarily located in rural areas and agricultural states. The life and survival of these churches are the descendants of its founders. However, due to technological advancements, improvement of highways, and the modernization of these communities, many of these churches will be forced to merge or close their doors.

Many of these churches—Mom-and-Pop and family churches—do not have trained and dedicated ministers. Many of these houses of worship lack the resources to attract qualified ministers. Most trained ministers are no longer interested in being called to a bi-vocational assignment. In other words, congregations of a digital society will need to be competitive when it comes to comfortability, accessibility, and practicality of the truth that it proclaims.

A shift in paradigm as it relates to church planting is taking place within the non-hierarchal denominations. Larger congregations are taking over smaller congregations that can no longer sustain themselves. Some of these larger congregations have church campuses throughout the United States and sometimes they have multiple campuses within a city. Most mega-congregations have more than one location or worship service. Some mega-congregations have locations that have a local pastor. There are churches actually looking to take over smaller congregations for the sole purpose of establishing presence in an area.

On the other hand, small churches must be able to attract members who have sufficient means. Churches are like public schools: the material earnings and investment of parents can impact the outcome of a child's education. Thus, the individual wealth of members invested in congregational ministries can impact faith seekers. Not all but most small churches do not have members that can give a five- or three-hundred-dollar tithe each Sunday. Consequently, smaller churches will not have the carnal resources to meet their practical needs: mortgage note, utilities, transportation, salaries, insurances, etc.

In the next twenty-five years (by 2041), most of the baby boomers will be deceased or too feeble to participate in church activities. Thus, for the most part, the church participants will consist of Generation X, the Millennial generation, and Generation "D" children. These generations of church members will not be loyal to denominations or congregations. For the most part, their attraction to a congregation will be based upon their relationships with persons other than Jesus Christ or the secular amenities of a congregation. According to church statisticians, Generation X and Millennials will unite with at least three different congregations and/or denominations during their lifetime. Generation "D" children have not been officially classified by church statisticians. It is my labeling for the next generation that will change the landscape of humanity ethos. This generation came into existence with the normalizing of the social-media platform. However, its full impact upon society will not be realized until the year of 2041.

Therefore, a small congregation's mission and purpose has to be front-and-center to survive the changing tides of the religious landscape. A *small congregation* is defined as a membership between two hundred and five hundred weekly attendees. The small congregation can grow and be relevant but it will require an understanding of its purpose. The purpose of a small congregation will be to involve humanity in the act of the personal touch as society moves to an impersonal norm. The small congregation has to be able to make available some digital platforms without sacrificing personal involvement. Finally, I believe, not exclusively, that small congregations will have the best opportunities to challenge humanity's decaying moral values both inside and outside of the worship centers, houses of worship, or churches.

G. OTHER CHURCH GROWTH RESOURCES

Cornelius, Bil, and Bill Easum. *Go BIG: Lead Your Church to Explosive Growth*. Nashville, Tennessee: Abingdon Press, 2006.

Easum, William M. *The Church Growth Handbook*. Nashville, Tennessee: Abingdon Press, 1990.

Harvey, Michael, and Rebecca Paveley. *Unlocking the Growth: You'll Be Amazed at Your Church's Potential*. Grand Rapids, MI: Monarch Books, 2012.

McIntosh, Gary L. *Biblical Church Growth: How You Can Work with God to Build a Faithful Church*. Grand Rapids, MI: Baker Books, 2003.

Searcy, Nelson, Kerrick Thomas, and Steve Sjogren. *Launch: Starting a New Church from Scratch*. Ventura, California: Regal Books, 2007.

H. OTHER BOOKS BY THE AUTHOR

Barlow, Calvin C., Jr. *C. J. Goes Hunting for Nouns*. Nashville, Tennessee: Lowbar Publishing Company, 2012.

—————. *Grace: Building Wealth One Penny at a Time*. Nashville, Tennessee: Lowbar Publishing Company, 2011.

—————. *Prophetic Building: A Nightmare or Vision*. Nashville, Tennessee: Relevant Publishing, 2006.

—————. *Preparing Your Church for Pastoral Leadership*. Nashville, Tennessee: Lowbar Publishing Company, 2009.

www.ingramcontent.com/pod-product-compliance
Lightning Source LLC
Chambersburg PA
CBHW070548300426
44113CB00011B/1825